CW00481691

Acknowledgements

I dedicate this book to my Grandad Sid, Grandad Jim and Nan Violet May Reeves (Hilda as me and my Sister nicknamed her) who all loved horses and a little flutter now and again and they were pleased I did a job that I loved and was passionate about even though they did not get to see me as much as they would have liked. But I know they were happy for me.

I would like to thank my good friend Amy whom without starting my 13th job I would never have met. I'm so grateful for this because it was she whom encouraged me to write down my life experiences working with horses.

I would also like to thank my Mum, Susan Fleming for proof reading my book, and Jazz my riding out buddy for taking the cover photo and allowing me to use it.

Contents page

Chapter 1.   Was it Fate or Something Else?

How My Race Career Began

In The Beginning:

I wasn't always in a an equine related job, my first was on a Youth Training Scheme (YTS) in the motor repair industry where I helped out at a garage doing tyre and exhaust fitting. I learned to repair tyres with punctures and use weights to balance them. But after a short while I realised it wasn't for me. I tried my hand for a bit at sheet metal work, and here I was taught how to use a lathe to make rollers and spindles (being the repair parts for service station kitchen cleaning equipment). But then fate took a hand.

I went to see a physic artist, she sat me down at her dining chair and sat opposite me. Instead of making notes in a book, she used a piece of A4 white paper and a charcoal pencil. Whilst chatting she started drawing and within a few minutes the whole page was covered in drawings. I remember seeing there was a field and within it was a tree on the right hand side, a Robin was perched on a branch and a horse was standing in the centre. She explained that the tree represented the tree of life, and, as it was a tall tree it meant I would live a long life. The Robin represented luck, and the horse in the field showed I would become a horse rider.

Although I was sceptical at first, little did I know back then that my next job would be as predicted. Quite soon after that reading, I applied and got my next job which was horse related. Maybe it was just all a coincidence, and that she put the idea into my mind; or was it fate, or something else? Whatever the reason I'm glad things turned out the way they did, because it was then that I felt I had at last found my vocation.

[Hereinafter, I mention equine-related terminology that some may be unfamiliar with. Rather than explain these in the main text of the book I have provided a definition and information section 'Equine jargon explained', as a separate last chapter.]

Chapter 2.   Finding My True Vocation

My First Horse-Related Job

How I got the Position:

At my interview the lady owner commented I was the only person, out of all those she had interviewed, who had stroked the dogs. Nothing much you might think but from this she could see I had a connection with animals. I believe that small act of kindness, a very natural thing for me to do, tipped the scales and landed me the job. It showed me there is more to a job interview than competence alone.

This livery yard was all about Dressage and Hunting. It was located in the countryside just outside of Bungay, a town in Norfolk. My duties here included grooming Dressage Horses in preparation for Eventing; and the exercising of Hunters in readiness for Hunting events. As the livery was 20 miles from my home it meant living-in with the family who owned the yard. Although I missed my family it was an adventure, and I soon settled in as I was made very welcome.

My first role was as a Stablehand doing manual chores such as mucking out stables, keeping the yard clean and tidy, as well as grooming the horses and preparing the their feeds. I also learnt how to ride a horse properly, and the lady owner taught me how to jump selected horses over horizontal bars (poles).

After just a short while she promoted me to Yard Manager with the responsibility of looking after the horses and other stable staff. I was now managing the wellbeing of horses and people.

As well as the general chores I also enjoyed helping to care for 3 ponies, 2 Hunters, an Arab Dressage horse, whom I would have loved to race as he was fast as lightning!

And not forgetting a shire horse called Badger. Badger was a huge horse measuring 18 hands (6 foot/1.829 meters tall). I would gallop him round a stubble field which was really fun. The bosses daughter would take him hunting and he could jump a six-foot iron gate effortlessly, he was an amazing jumper.

I had some other enjoyable experiences at this livery, including:

1. Going on the hunt was also an enjoyable part of this job for me, and I was grateful to my boss for allowing me to take part. We didn't see one fox during any of the times I joined them (only one large badger) which I was secretly pleased about.

2. Practicing Dressage maneuvers on the Arab horse. I would take him in the horse-box to an indoor ménage about 30 minutes drive away. Here, I was privileged to be taught this skill by a lady instructor from Germany. She said I was at one with my horse, and think she was telling me the horse responded well to my riding because he felt safe and trusted me.

3. I also looked after my first racehorse here. The owner bought him from the sales hewas aptly called 'Special Offer'.

4. Another race horse here was a dark bay mare and she could be a bit of a naughty horse and I often wondered if the saying, " so and so was being a right mare," originated from looking after mischievous horses. Still I got on really well with this mare and she became quite calm with me. I was the only one she would let groom and place a rug on; so I took charge of looking after her and grooming her which duly strengthened that bond. Sadly we only looked after her for a few months whilst she was having a rest from her Newmarket racing yard. I felt sad to see her go and missed that special connection we had and I think the mare felt sad as well. Animals are said to be a good judge of human character, some would even say better than humans are.

The time came to move on as I really wanted to join a racing yard.

Chapter 3.   From Norfolk to Sussex

My First Racehorse Role

In The Money:

My first Racehorse related role, was at a racing yard, located in Sussex. This stable was a good move for me. It had reached third in the top trainers list that year achieving 99 wins.

It was in this job I received my first pool money for those wins. Stable hands would be given a bonus, every quarter (being a percentage of the horses winnings, or placements). I remember personally receiving about three month's worth of salary after one quarter. This was a considerable amount of money for a low paid stablehand.

As well as the normal daily chores, mucking out, grooming and general care, it was here I first learned to ride racehorses, a very different experience to Dressage. I rode a 12-year-old grey gelding who had won many races over the years but had been retired, but not completely as his new role was to support the training of novice riders.

He was a tall horse approximately 17 hands, (5' 8''/1.727m). I remember how I first had to learn to jump up onto the grey before I could ride him. I was a slip of a lad at 17, weighing under 8 stone and not tall. It was a long way up to jump but I managed after a number of attempts and after overcoming some challenges. One being the other lads having a laugh on me, making a clicking noise near the grey, causing him spook and run away with me. It was all done in good humour as part of my training learning curve.

Although the other lads enjoyed a laugh at my expense they were also good to me. During our meal breaks, because I had never ridden racehorses before, they helped me learn how to ride bareback, no saddle just a bridal, on a pony; and also how to keep my balance when taking the pony over jumps, also bareback. They used a simple but effective method of mentoring. They would put a matchbox under each of my knees and I had to keep them in place. This was a useful tip for gripping with the knees effectively to support balance and staying on the horse, so a key skill in riding.

It was well worth the effort and persevering to get my challenges conquered because over the time I learned to ride the grey horse well. I was able to take him up the gallops last thing, after the other horses had gone which was better for me as I didn't have to worry that he would keep trying to run off. It's hard to explain how when you ride racehorses it seems one day you can't hold them and then one day, suddenly, you learn the knack of handling them. Somehow it just clicks and happens naturally, which makes sense of this equestrian quote, "*Racehorse riding is 5% strength and 95% knack*".

Other duties at this yard included driving, such as taking horse boxes to the races. Two horses in my care, won races; One horse cost hundreds of thousands as a yearling when bought by a rich Arab owner. This winning horse had really good breeding, his wins included attaining a second 'by a short head', and also a win 'by a short head'. Sadly, I alone took him to the sales at Newmarket where sadly he was sold for a much smaller amount.

A few days later my boss received a letter from a lady who was also selling a horse at the same sale. Her letter conveyed to my boss that the horse had behaved impeccably with me and I was a credit and an asset to his yard. She also wrote out of concern, advising that whilst I was away during my lunch and another lad had taken over my duties. This time the horse had behaved really badly with that lad who was seen to be knocking the horse about. She said she didn't mention it to me when I got back as she thought I might have been upset that my horse had been mistreated whilst I was gone.

I was saddened about the cruelty from the other lad but very touched someone took the time to write about the event, and commending me to my boss regarding my good behavior and my compassion for horses. I have kept this letter and used it a number of times as a reference since then when attending job interviews.

Of the two other horses I cared for, one also won races but sadly the other horse never raced but I believe he would have made a good riding horse for someone.

It was whilst in this role, I met a top Flat Jockey, who only rode in flat races and not over jumps. He was several times a champion jockey and rode a number of the horses belonging to my boss, including one horse I was privileged to ride and care for. He was champion miler (a horse who runs over the distance of one mile).

I have some very happy memories and learned much about horses and grooming work in this short time. I was only at this yard about a year as decided to leave and find a job nearer to my family.

Chapter 4.   A Change is as Good as a Rest

My First 'Flat' and 'Jump' Yard

My Favourites:

My first 'flat and jump 'yard was at a stable in Yorkshire with a lady racehorse trainer. My role here included grooming and general horse care such as learning how to plait a horse's main. Other duties were exercising horses, including riding them at a gallop in readiness for racing, and driving the horse-box transporting horses to and from the races.

It was here that I found my first favourite racehorse. I nicknamed her Miss A, she was a five year old, dark bay, about 15 hands. This mare would whinny when I came walking up the the yard to see her. She was so sweet and gentle, I could hold a polo mint between my lips and she would gently take it from me. This racehorse ran 86 times and won 5 races on the flat and was second 6 times, and third 11 times. She only ran once over hurdles at Bangor on Dee. She wasn't a jumper though as not bred for that, rather she was a 6-furlong on the flat racehorse. Hence not unexpectedly she did not get the trip/distance. The distance she would have needed to cover was over a mile and a half on the flat to achieve 2 miles over hurdles. This would have required her to have lots of stamina workouts, prior, which she didn't have.

At York race course, we would prepare the horses by exercising them at a gallop on the far side of the track, where there was approximately a 5 furlong gallop length. I rode my favourite Miss A on the gallops here before her races. She was very strong and powerful and to keep control of the ride I would need to pull my irons up really short.

[to control a strong horse and stop it running off with its rider, foot irons are set shorter than normal. The shorter the irons the better, as this allows the rider to lean back in the saddle with feet forward and to gain a good secure hold of the reigns.]

Miss A became really attached to me and we seemed to have a really good bond. I believe horses do get attached to people who look after them. Once, when I got back from a two week holiday, I was told she missed me and hadn't eaten well. Happily very soon after my return she was back to her normal self. Her prize money totalled many thousands of pounds, before she was put to foal; I like to imagine her foals became fine race winners too.

Other fun privileges at this yard included, being lucky enough to lead up a jump horse that won at Cheltenham, and, looking after a two year old racehorse that ran in a big race at Redcar Called 'The Tote 2 year old Trophy Race', he finished third. I had to wear a white jacket with the race name printed on it which I kept from all those years ago and still have to this day.

Some accolades I personally received at this yard included, 'Best Turned Out 'prize at Ascot races for having my horse plaited and well-groomed. I also received £250 and a glass tankard, etched with a navy ship in its own presentation box (again a treasured memory and a keepsake).

I remained in this yard very happily for several years before moving on to my next job, for financial reasons.

Chapter 5.   Life's a Beach

Short and Sweet Jersey

Island Life:

My next job was on the lovely island of Jersey, this time working for a male Racehorse trainer. I saw the position advertised in the Racing Post a horse-racing paper. As I had many happy memories of holidaying in Jersey as a child it appealed to me to revisit. The interview consisted of a phone chat with the owner/trainer who invited me to come to Jersey and try out the role.

Here, my duties consisted of feeding, grooming and exercising the horses, as well as general horse care.

Highlights included riding out on a weekend with a lovely lady who was an auntie of a famous jump jockey nicknamed 'Chocolate'. She was a very interesting lady and it was nice listening to the stories she told about him.

Another perk was actually living on Jersey where:
(i) I was able to cycle down to the beach on my days off,
(ii) there was zero tax on purchases. At the time I smoked and I remember 20 cigarettes were only £3.50, which was cheap then, and
(iii)   my wages weren't taxed which was another bonus even though it was only for 6 weeks.

It was a a real pleasure working on this idyllic island but it wasn't to be. I believe another staff member pressured my boss to let me go. It had been mentioned to me earlier, in passing, that this employee was worried. That he feared I might be given preferential treatment regarding race rides due to my small build and low weight. It was a shame but a lesson in life learnt, and I have no regrets it was a great experience for me.

Hence, this job lasted a mere six weeks and although a very nice job all round it was, sadly, 'short but sweet'.

Chapter 6: Once Bitten Twice Shy

Returning to Yorkshire

It's Never the Same:
My next horse role was to return to the lady trainer mentioned in Chapter four, where this time around my duties consisted of attending the race days, galloping racehorses in preparation for races, and general day to day horse care.

One of the perks of working for this yard were the numerous 'Jump and Flat' winners it produced. This was great for everyone including the stablehands because they received good-sized bonuses, from a share in the 'Pool Money' out of the racehorse winnings.

One horse I looked after and rode was a light-bay gelding of about 17 hands whom I nicknamed Spike, because he had a tufty forelock (just above his forehead). He was a gentle and sweet natured horse, easy to control and a pleasure to ride. I took him to a number of racecourses such as Plumpton, Leicester, Huntingdon, Warwick, and also further afield to Taunton, where he won.

As a wise person once told me, "Never go back to were you worked before it's never the same", and sadly that person was

right, it wasn't the same. Miss A had gone as put to foal, and although I heard she did have a foal, there were no other details after that. Sadly another horse, a favourite of mine, died under anesthetic whilst having a leg operation. Another life lesson learned and hence I only stayed there for two years. However, I kept in touch and visited the yard from time to time when I later worked at a neighboring Yorkshire yard. Here I boarded with a most lovely landlady, Sheila, whose lodgings were just a few hundred yards from this 'Jump and Flat' yard.

Chapter 7:   Love Them or Hate Them

Working with Arab Racehorses

Up a Notch:

My next job was with a lady Arabian racehorse trainer. It was in the countryside in a lovely part of Sussex. It was a family run yard, with Arabian racehorses and a couple of Arabian mares which the family would breed from. This would be a change of pace and working with a very different breed of racehorse.

I believe I was fortunate to be chosen for this job because of my perceived riding skill. At my interview I was asked to ride a small chestnut Arab mare, nicknamed Sunny. This was over the lady's gallops which was a flat track at the side of a field to give a horse a fast gallop ride, and was about 6 furlongs long (8 furlongs is a mile/1.608Km).

This mare was very strong and reminded me of my favourite Miss A, at the Yorkshire yard. I controlled her well and held her at a steady canter. I was really pleased when told I was the only one, out of all the people interviewed, that could ride that horse well, and hold her steady. It was right there and then I was told, "You have a job".

Some perks whilst at this yard included:

1. I continued to exercise the chestnut Arab mare, and was pleased when she won some Arab races whilst I was there. And I enjoyed going to the races, and the thrill of riding and galloping these horses.

2. Arab racehorse were also bred at this yard, and this provided an extra bit of variety in this job, a side of racing I hadn't seen before.

3. It was here that I was given the opportunity to do an 'Arab Jockey' course at Lingfield Race Course which would then enable me to ride in Arab races. Part of this course included a mock race and controlling the horse during typical race conditions consisting of

(i) a race 'false start' and getting the horse calm and back into a starting position

(ii) a race 're-start'. A tape had been drawn across the track, and the horse placed behind it. On signal the tape was let go, and the trainee jockeys were off, racing each other to the winning post, which was about five furlongs (just over half a mile) in distance. My horse came third although I believe we could have won. Earlier my boss had asked me to be easy on this mare as she was to run an actual race soon. I brought her in third and fortunately still got a pass, for which I received my Arab Jockey Licence. Sadly though I didn't get an opportunity to race but the experience was very worthwhile and taught me a lot.

Ending on a positive note, the mare I trained on at the jockey course won the mentioned race straight after the trial race. I understood then that my boss was wise to ask me to hold her back. She won further races for us and I was happy to have been a part of that success.

I continued at this yard for about another year before looking to my next challenge.

Chapter 8:   Spooky Steep Hills

The Oxford Job

Not All Experience is Good:

My next job experience was at a hunt and livery yard again set in the countryside, this time close to Oxford, working for a lady livery yard owner. It was a family run business some 40 miles from home and so I lived in as part of the family.

As well as the general stable and care part of my role, my additional duties included attending point to point racing days locally such as at Mollington, Kingston Blount and Siddington. To keep the horses fit for hunting and point to point racing the horses would be regularly exercised, known as work riding.

I enjoyed riding out, and exercising of both 'flat' and 'jump' horses. We sometimes did 4 gallop sessions in a day on 4 different horses, one after the other. With another lad, who was a jump jockey, we would ride two horses to the gallops and work ride them for about 20 mins. In the meantime two girls from the yard would follow us there with two more horses. When we had galloped the first two the trainer would swap over the horses leaving us a new pair to exercise and the girls would take the first pair back, repeating till we had galloped 8 horses.

Part of the exercise routine was to take the horses on a regular hack. Which consisted entering a field, where the area partly was banked on both sides. We would take the horses down one side, and at the bottom there was a stream. In summer the water would be mostly dried up, with just a few puddles of water remaining. From there we would go up the other side of the bank, quite a steep hill, to get back onto the flat.

One particular day, I was riding a horse, one inclined to rear up for no apparent reason, and on this particular day, as we went up the steep hill my horse got scared. Something had spooked him and he suddenly reared up and fell over backwards taking me down with him. Once down he instinctively went to get up, and fortunately, I managed to get my feet out of the stirrups and jump out of his way.

He had landed on his back and luckily not harmed himself, or me. At the time, it was quite a scary experience as it was the first time anything like that had happened to me. The experience must have really shaken him too, because after that day he was a really nice calm ride. He never reared over backwards again, and wasn't naughty again, after that one shocking experience.

I enjoyed my time at this yard going to the races, work riding the horses, and caring for the horses. Sadly I was only at this yard for a year as the trainer moved to Devon.

Chapter 9:   Onwards and Upwards

From Stable Lad to Yard Manager

A New Nickname:
I made the decision not to go Devon in preference to stay more locally, and joined a yard with a racehorse trainer, near Newbury. The yard was located in a racing town not far from Newbury town centre, one of several training yards in the area.

Here, my duties as well as the normal horse care and exercise included work riding the horses, feeding each horse according to individual requirements as well as checking their feet and legs, plus general management of the yard and yard staff. This also entailed taking the horses to the races, looking after and caring for/grooming the horses at race locations, and putting them into the stalls for the for the jockeys, ready for the start of the race.

It was here I got the nickname 'The Cat'. This was because I had taught myself to ride, sitting aerodynamically low to the saddle, copying the American jockey style of riding. Which meant when I jumped out of the stalls my body was crouch-like as a cat ready to pounce. Normally a UK jockey would sit more upright.

My boss at this yard was pleased with my knowledge, the way I worked, and rode, and the way I turned out the horses for races. Soon he made me Head Lad, which meant when he wasn't there I was placed in charge of the yard, managing the staff and ensuring the yard was kept clean and tidy. A big part of the role was the proper care of the horses. Importantly, each evening, the horses legs would be checked for swelling after their daily workout, and for any cuts or other damage to the legs or body and treating as necessary; and generally making sure they remained sound and fit to race.

Part of general day to day care was making up individual horse feeds and ensuring these were distributed efficiently. It is very important that each horse receives the right amount of feed for its daily needs depending on its size and the amount of work/exercise the horse is regularly doing. Getting it wrong can cause the horse all sorts of problems. If they get too little feed this could result in demineralization of bones in mature horses and general fatigue. On the other hand if overfed the risks are many such as digestive problems, ulcers, colic and unhealthy weight gain. These can lead to more serious conditions such as obesity, behavioral issues, and ailments such as laminitis and colic, both of which can cause fatalities if not corrected quickly.

Another important role was preparing the horse-racing equipment in readiness for races. This included preparing the 'horse-racing gear' and ready the horse for racing, on race days. *[A list of typical race items to be prepared can be found in last Chapter which covers equestrian terms and other information]*

Race Days:

The race items for the jockey would be placed in a colour bag (a leather satchel) to given to the weight room at a specified time before the race (the weight room is a place where the jockey is weighed before and after each race). The colour bag contains the owner's racing colours for the jockey to wear, a saddle pad, and a non-slip pad (chamois). The jockey's valet would normally supply the saddle and girths for the jockey. At weigh in, all the above are carried by the jockey who stands on the weigh-in scales. The weigh-in is important because it is used for equalizing the weight of both riders and horses.

Another race-related duty was to train a number horses to go through the racing stalls. This consisted of practicing the drill, reassuring them till they were comfortable in the stalls, and confident to run quickly forward out of the stalls when the two gates suddenly opened. This practice was repeated a number of times to get the horses used to the start procedures and not be startled by the gates opening or by any associated noise. I was very pleased when one of the horses I trained through the racing stalls, won a race. It was just a few days after finishing her schooling, she won with impressive odds, coming in at a whopping 66-1. Unfortunately I hadn't bet on her, as I wasn't at the races that day, as back home managing the yard.

I enjoyed my time at this yard and gained a lot of knowledge about running a yard and getting horses and gear ready for racing. However, Yorkshire was tugging at my heart strings and it was time to move on.

Chapter 10.   It's A Knockout

Yorkshire Beckons:

My next venture took me back to Yorkshire, set in the countryside a few miles outside of York. This time returning to a 'Jump and Flat' training yard, another family owned business. As this was about 150 miles from home I boarded with a couple about 5 miles from the yard.

It was here that part of my duties included riding-out horses that raced on the 'flat' and over 'hurdles/jump racing', and exercised them on the gallops, plus the general horse care, feeding, grooming, plaiting and pulling mains.

At this yard we would weigh the horses once a week, before and after their races to see how much weight they had lost, and record the results. This was helpful information for the horse's trainer for keeping an eye on the horses weight, as well as providing an indication as to the right amount of feed to give them (correct feeding habits is important for the health and wellbeing of horses as described more fully in the last chapter).

After a short time, I was made up to Travelling Head Lad. In this promoted role, my duties consisted of driving the horse box to the races and leading them up at the races.

When at the races I would groom the horse about one hour and twenty minutes before the race, put on a bridle and a lead reign and walk it around the pre-parading ring for about thirty minutes (some race courses are too small for a pre-parading ring in which case the horses are walked about the stable yard). Around ten minutes before the race the trainer would saddle up the horse ready for the jockey. Then the horse would then be taken to the parade ring and walked around for about ten minutes for the crowd to view and study.

The jockey would enter the parade ring about 10 minutes before the race to talk to the trainer and receive his race instructions. About 5 minutes before the race, the trainer would give the jockey a leg-up (that is they would hold the jockeys left leg and the jockey would use this support to jump onto the horse), and then I would take off the lead reign while walking them round. It was then my role to lead the horse and jockey onto the race course. Shortly after this walk to get the horses accustomed to having a rider on their back, they would cantered down to the start, and then put into the stalls in number order (the number of the stall the horse runs from is based on a random draw done earlier).

Stepping Up:

One new and important farrier task I learnt at this yard was due directly to something that happened one race day.

There was an incident were a horse, from a large yard, had been running in a big race. During that race a shoe had come loose and the shoe nail had punctured the horse's foot. The shoe needed taking off, immediately, but there wasn't a farrier available to do this. There was no one else who knew how to do this safely. Sadly due to the delay in attending to this injury, the horse got a foot infection and the foot was so damaged the horse never raced again.

What happened to this horse was due to the lack of knowledge of those around on that race day. This was motivation for me to learn how to take a horses shoe off correctly and safely, so I could make sure this would never happen to any horses in my care.

Another learning opportunity during my time at this yard was to study the veterinary side of horse care, which included how to administer injections, take horses bloods, and also on several occasions I got the chance to endoscopy the horses. This entails putting a scope up the horses nostrils, to then wait for them to breathe at which time an opening appears through oesophagus which enables you to push the scope through into the stomach. Scoping is a way to check for good breathing and also to look for other underlying illnesses, such as ulcers, tumors, polyps, and other upper Gastrointestinal [GI], tract abnormalities.

It's a Knockout:
Daily, the horses would be exercised on the gallops. The gallops here were 3 furlongs (just under 1/2 a mile) on the flat and then uphill for 2 furlongs (1/4 of a mile). The ride would consist of a canter along the flat and up hill, then to turn around and canter back down the hill steadily.

On one particular day I was riding a 'jump' horse on the gallops. Which was going fine until we were on the way back, down the hill. My horse stumbled, throwing me over his head, accidentally kicking me in the stomach, and then standing on my leg.I was momentarily knocked out and dreaming I was at home in my bed. When I came round I was laid face down on the track and the horse had gone, it had made its way back to the yard by itself, fortunately for him he was non-the-worse for his fall.

However, I wasn't so lucky, it had been a bad fall for me. I still have the imprint of the horses hoof on my left leg, 12 years on.

Also where the horse fell on me it damaged some nerves in my leg, which at the time I didn't realise would take some 10 years before any feeling returned to it. Although I considered myself lucky not to have been seriously hurt, and I was able to return to work after only 3 days of recovery, my confidence was knocked badly. So much so, a few days later, I decided to call it a day and made the very sad decision to leave racing and try a different type of job.

Chapter 11.   The Twelve Year Gap

A Different Track

The Indoor Life:
 Considering an indoor role was a complete change for me after the fast pace of racing and being outdoors. My early plan was to learn how to be a plumber, and to take that up as a skilled career move, and to eventually have my own business. But as often is the case, things don't always to go plan.

 I had moved back to Norfolk and couldn't find any suitable college classes or any plumbers looking for a trainee. But needs must, and I started work for a large DIY store, in the warehousing division. It was only ever going to be temporary but one year merged into the next and the suddenly 10 years had passed. I did however, do a written plumbing course, via remote learning, which came in useful for answering DIY questions from customers. I built up quite a nice clientele of regulars who would ask for my help and advice.

 Yet, despite the years passing, the equestrian life was never far from my mind. One day I was talking to a work colleague who commented that I didn't look happy in the role and asked what job I had done before this one. I explained, I used to work in the horse racing industry taking care of Racehorses, and escorting them to various different racecourses up and down the country. She surprised me by saying that maybe I should try this again as it made me happy being around horses.

 It didn't take much to get me thinking, perhaps she was right and that I wasn't happy where I was. Her comment brought back many memories of those happy days. So much so that just out of curiosity, I told myself, I found and wrote to a few trainers enclosing my CV. I was very pleased when I got a reply from a lady Racehorse Trainer, at a yard not far from where I was currently living.

On my next weekend off, I arranged to go for an interview. As part of the interview I was asked to show my riding skills by cantering one of her horses, which I later nicknamed Dude. It was a circle gallop about 3 furlongs round. The ride consisted of three canters in one direction and three in the other direction. Followed by a walk round the circle to cool the horse off before unsaddling and washing him down, before putting him back into his stable.

What a buzz that was, I had gotten the bug and didn't want it to end. I had forgotten how much I had enjoyed riding and it all came back in an instant. I asked if I could ride another, and she agreed. This time the Trainer put me on a 'jump' horse, he was about 17 hands (5'8"/1.727m) high. This horse was quite strong but I managed to keep control of him despite not having ridden for so long, my experience had automatically kicked in.

After riding the jump horse I watched a few horses go round the gallops, before making my leave. But, to my complete surprise the Owner/Trainer offered me a job right there and then. Unbeknown to me, she had noticed me stroking, and speaking nicely to the horses whilst I was waiting to be interviewed. I think this might have helped swing her decision to say yes to me working for her yard. I went home feeling very happy indeed.

I wasted no time and immediately handed in my notice and said goodbye to the DIY business. Yeh! after more than a decade I was back in the racing industry.

Chapter 12. Returning to My Passion

Home Is Where the Heart Is

Back in the Saddle:

I'm so glad, my work colleague made that one suggestion which led to me to make the decision to apply for, and take the initial steps to get back into racing. I feel it has made me a much better person, as I'm happier in myself and doing the work I'm passionate about, working with racehorses again.

Yeh! I was back in racing with a lovely lady boss who respected me for my knowledge and compassion for racehorses. There were many enjoyable experiences to come. Also, when seeing my family and friends on race days and when they visited me at the yard, where they could see how happy I was in my work and also witnessed my love of horses.

Working with horses has provided me much happiness. I have always felt horses temperaments are just like peoples, in that you instantly warm to some horses more than others. As I mentioned earlier, we do tend to have our favourites. Although I loved them all there have been some more cherished. In particular were three mares, one gelding, and my most favoured gelding, one that I transported to the races and lead up. Here are some reasons why they were dearest since returning to racing.

Dude

The first horse was the one I rode during my job interview, the one I later nicknamed Dude. Dude a gelding, was lovely to ride, as very good-natured. I felt lucky to have a part in caring for him and training him. Riding him out on the gallop, helping him to be fit and ready for the races he ran.

I felt that special connection with Dude when I first met him and pretty soon this developed into a strong bond of understanding with him. Each morning I would put my hand on his cheek and he seemed to like that, and this made me happy too. Although Dude was later retired he remained at the yard cared for, in his old age, by the Trainer's family. This was lovely as it meant I could continue to visit him.

Dude remains my all time favourite gelding to ride, perhaps partly as he was the first horse I rode on my return back into racing, and him being part and parcel of the adrenaline that flowed through me that interview day. Although, there was one incident that could have resulted in a very different perception of him altogether.

Dude

Krackpot

My most favourite racehorse to lead up was nicknamed, Krackpot who had a number of wins, as well as coming in second and third, after just a few months of joining the yard, and one a few more since. The owner has seen much improvement from this Racehorse, since his move here and that is nice to hear.

Krackpot was the best horse for leading up at the races. I was especially fond of him after being privileged to lead him on one of his winning occasions. He was such a pleasure

To lead up and groom. He also liked to be fussed but this wasn't

always the case it took a while and patience for him to warm towards receiving affection and being hugged.

Krackpot

Whirly-B

My much-cherished 4-year-old mare is one I called Whirly-B. Again, I felt a strong connection with her the very first time I saw her. Every morning when in work, I would make it a habit to visit Whirly-B to give her a quick hug and kiss her cheek. I like to

think she knew I cared for her as she would always come to the stable door when I called her.

Also, if she saw me cuddling other horses I got the feeling she gave me funny looks, and I believed she did get a bit jealous. Sometimes she was a bit mischievous too, for example, when I groomed her she would try to move close to me, so as to squash me between herself and the wall. On these occasions I would place my hand on her cheek and the other on her neck or shoulder, whilst talking to her gently. After just a few minutes she would calm down. I put those naughty tricks down to her way of getting some extra attention from me, which of course worked every time.

AOF

The horse I enjoyed to ride most was one of my three favourite mares nicknamed AOF , She had won a number of races as well as achieved second and third places. AOF was a pleasure to ride because she would always do everything you asked of her, she was always calm to ride and never attempted to buck you off the saddle.

AOF loved to be cuddled but as good natured as she was she too could be a bit naughty when being brushed. Sometimes she would try to squash me against her and the wall and on occasion would go to nip me but not nasty, more in a playful way. But these traits didn't stop me loving her to bits, as overall she was a delight to care for.

Aof

Kissy Cas
        The second of the mares much loved, I called Kissy Cas. She's was a 4-year-old who also loved her cuddles and kisses. She was my secret favourite girlie just between her and me. She too won races as well as getting second and third places. I was

particularly fond of Kissy Cas as I had led her up for two of her wins. I like to believe she was as fond of me as I of her.

Wiggy
        My best boy whom was known by his nickname Wiggy, ran around a 100 times, winning numerous races as well as many second and third placings. His prize money reflected his achievements. Wiggy had reached a good age of 11 years but it wasn't obvious as he looked so well and fit. Wiggy as a semi-retired, gelding racehorse was used to support the young horses on

the canter and gallop exercises. He loved being ridden, and now with the added bonus of getting lots of time out in the fields, he had a wonderful life.

Wiggy

Out of the Saddle

Unfortunately, my return to racing took a bit of a downturn due to an accident in my first year at this yard. This resulted in a bad fall whilst out riding, only my second in a long career of riding.

I was out on Dude when something spooked him. This made him put in a huge buck, which projected me to one side, I was forcibly thrown off and landed on concrete. This fall resulted in the ripping my 'piriformis' muscle in my leg which I was advised was considered worse than breaking a bone as muscle takes longer to recover.

This accident made me feel really sad as the thought of not being able to ride again was devastating to me. It was my life and my passion, I could not think of a life without the joy of riding. I believe the thought of losing what I loved doing, and having lost it once before, made me all the more determined to get my self fit and well, and to push myself to get back riding.

And Back in the Saddle

I am quietly proud of myself for enduring the necessary programme of fitness that got me back to being fit to ride again. It took 12 weeks of rest and further weeks (4 months in total) to bring my fitness back to the necessary standards for riding thoroughbreds.

Fortunately, I was insured for such an event and was able to take the timeout needed for my recovery. I am also most grateful to my employer for having the patience during the long recovery time, when I couldn't work, and for keeping my job open despite the long gap. My reward for my early patience and then a strict fitness regime, was to be able to ride racehorses again, to get them fit to race, and gallop them ready for races (the fun bit).

Race Days:
    My role on a race-day would consist of driving the horse-box to transport horses and staff to the racecourse venue, and leading horses up at the races as well as looking after their general care whilst away from the yard. More on this in the next chapter.

Additional Experience:
    My role on a Raceday when not attending the races, was as racing manager (getting the horses race gear ready). I also held the position of second head lad which involved being in charge of the horses, staff and yard, in the absence of the boss and head lad.This was in additional to my yard manager role, with responsibilities for keeping the yard clean and tidy, and maintaining the general good appearance of the yard.

Learning & Development:
    I was given the opportunity to attend a 2-day amateur riders course in 2019, by way of a glowing reference from my boss. I was very grateful for her confidence in me. This course was one of the routes to become an amateur jockey, with the certification to ride in amateur races. Whilst an amateur jockey taking part in amateur races is unpaid and limited to amateur race rides only, it's seen as a good stepping stone to become a professional jockey.

    The course consisted of 2 days at the British Racing School. Day One, included practice on a race horse simulator, which was as if riding on a real race course. Day Two, included a fitness test in the gym, outdoor exercises, and a practice session on jumping out of the stalls.

    Sadly I did not pass my amateur riders course as my fitness results let me down by a small margin. However, I enjoyed the experience and learnt a lot about myself mentally and physically. I learnt for example just how fit and strong jockeys need to be. With just a small percentage off a pass, I am proud I gave this a go, and feel privileged to have had the experience.

Best Laid Plans:
    This racing yard also bred Thoroughbred race horses, having several mares to breed from. When a horse gets

covered by a stallion it is scanned 16 days later to check if it was successful and that the mare is in foal. This was a very successful part of the yard's overall business.

However, in late November 2019 it became known that a global deadly, to humans, virus known as the Corona Virus (Corvid-19) had emerged in China. By March 2020 it had spread throughout the world.

Change Happens:
Every business has been touched by the effects of the virus. It very soon became obvious that new ways of working would become the new normal, for example more being done online and remotely. For any business that relies on human contact, equine related businesses for example, would have particular difficulties. Lockdown measures had been put in place with only essential business having the green light to continue.

Knock-on Effect:
Should racing be stopped, even for a limited time, the Thoroughbred horses who need regular exercise to keep them in prime condition for racing, would be significantly affected. With less intense race-ready exercise, it would change the dynamics of their previous form, some never regaining their earlier stamina.

Also, if there were no travel for mares to go to the stud in 2020. It would change the horse racing industry as we know it. There would be an ongoing gap if there were no yearlings for 2021 nor any sales of young horses. The future of racing could be seriously damaged as a result.

Chapter 13.   What Happens on a Race Day?

Preparation is Key

MUCH TO DO

Before any race day there is much preparation at the owners yard and then more, on reaching the race course itself.

At the Owner's Yard:

Race Day Additional duties would include putting together:
(i) the 'horse-racing gear' and ready the horse for racing, on race days the gear would consist of:
* bridal
* bucket and sponge
* Chifney bit
* head collar and rope
* lead reign
* paddock sheet
* sheet pad
* sheet roller
* sweat scraper
* sweat sheet for after the race
* tail bandage
* travel rug
* travel bandages
(ii) the racing gear for the saddle and jockey, which was made up of:
* chamois
* girth's (x2)
* racing colours for the jockey
* saddle pad
* visors/blinkers.

Readying the Horses for the Journey:

On the morning of the race, horses that are racing are exercised on the horse walker for 15 minutes. At 0700 the horse gets a set feed, and then is groomed for around thirty minutes before setting off for the races, in the horse-box. The departure time is based on the expected journey time plus a further two and a half hours rest time for the horses between arrival and their allocated run schedule.

At the Racecourse:

Entrance to the racecourse for attendants is by way of a stable pass card which is handed over on arrival to gain access to the stables. The attendees sign in and each racehorse's identity chip (microchip in their neck) is scanned, as a check that it's the correct horse. The horses are then allocated a stable. At this point we would ask for one with 'shavings as bedding' rather than other options such as 'paper or straw bedding', as horses tend to eat these types.

Once stables are sorted the horses are walked round for about 10 minutes, so as to stretch their legs after travelling in the box. After the walk they are then put into the prepared stable and given half a bucket of water. Roundabout an hour and a half before the horse's race the water is removed. The horse is then groomed, hooves picked out and oiled and quarter marks put on. Sometimes the horses mains will be plaited too.

Placing the Race Gear:

The racing bridle and a lead reign are put on and the horse is then taken for another walk round, for 20 minutes or so. Just prior to the race the trainer brings a saddle weight cloth and a non-slip pad, a saddle pad, girth and a surcingle.

The placement order goes like this:
1.   The non-slip pad is put on, followed by the saddle pad, then the number cloth.
2.   The saddle is placed.
3.   The girths are attached to the saddle and pulled up on both sides.
4.   The surcingle is put over the top of the girth and is tightened up. During this stage the   horses front legs are stretched forward so the girth adjustment does not pinch them underneath, (its under belly).

Last Minute Preparations:

Water is squirted into the horses mouth to hydrate them, 20 mins before they race. The horses are then taken to the parade ring, where the microchip is scanned again to make sure it is still the right horse for that race. The horses will then be walked round again for about 10 minutes, this time in the parade ring.

Almost Set:

Around the same time the jockeys enter the middle of the parade ring where they meet the trainer and owners, and it's here they receive their instructions for the race. The trainer and the jockey then go over to meet the horse. The trainer legs the jockey up onto the horse which is then led onto the race course. Here the jockey would then canter his horse down to the start where the stalls are, which the horse and jockey will enter in readiness to race. They then wait for their draw number to be called and then the horse is loaded into the stall, by the stall handler to await the start of the race.

Chapter 14. Life Lessons and Other Experiences

Challenges and Benefits

Here I share a little of what I've learned and what I have loved during my time in racing and some other experiences that might be of interest.

Love of Horses
If you love horses and are up for a challenge, I would highly recommend a career in horse racing care and management.Throughout my time in the racing community. One of the things I cherish is, having had the opportunity to learn to ride racehorses. This has allowed me to work in the racehorse industry and working with horses, my passion.

Learning the trade:
(a) Knowing how to judge the distance a horse needs to race and therefore run a horse over the right distance.
(b) Understanding the type of ground a horse prefers to race on such as, soft ground, good ground or fast ground. For example if a horse has a high knee action it usually likes soft ground.
(c) How to gallop them efficiently so as to get them fit and ready for racing, and to manage a suitable pace when taking them on the gallops, either upside another horse or alone.
(d) Learning how to take a horses shoe off safely should a problem occur and a farrier isn't on hand to do it. It's very important to the horses' welfare to do this correctly and not to damage the horses' hoof, in the process.

(e) How to take blood from a horse, also how to scope them, as well as how to administer injections to prevent illness.

Other training included the more mundane daily tasks such as:
1.   The proper use of a hoof pick before putting the horses on the walker. This was a daily morning task, mundane, yet essential for the horses wellbeing. The hoof pick has a number of important purposes.
- to pick from the horses hoof any dirt, stone or other object that might have gotten stuck in it (to prevent it going lame or cause other serious leg conditions such as infection)
- to check for loose or missing shoes
- to check if the horse has heat in it's legs (explained more fully in definitions)
- to see if the horses legs are sound, not cuts
2.   Driving the horse-box and transporting horses to and from the racecourses.
3.   To pull horses mains and plait them
4.   To do quarter marks on horses
5.   To understand the measurements used in racing circles, such as
- a horses height is measured in hands (1 hand = 4 inches). This is measured from the front hoof from the floor up to the withers.
- There are 8 furlongs in a mile (One furlong is an eighth of a mile/220yards).

Do Horses remember you? I found this answer really interesting

It is commonly believed that horses can read a human's facial expression and remember human emotions. For example, it is said that:
(i)   If you go into a horses stable smiling and happy, the horse can recognise your happy   facial expression and feels your positivity and positive energy.
(ii)   if you go into a horse stable for the first time with an angry face or in a bad mood the   horse perceives this facial expression, and feels the negativity and negative energy.
(ii)   The next time you greet the horse it remembers your happy or negative face.
(iii)   Horses use this recognition to determine whether the person is a threat or not.

The softer side of horse management

ALTERNATIVE HEALING

I started training in 2017, in my free time, the art of 'RIKI and SUKEME'. My teacher was a lady with over 20 years teaching experience. On completion of this training I received a certificate of qualification for equine, dog, and human healing.

I believe I am a natural healer, having empathy with the horses in my care (sometimes known as horse whispering). I feel I have a positive energy in my hands and this helps with healing. This energy is known as 'Dantian Healing'. Some clients have said they can feel this energy from me even before I touch them, describing it as like a faint pins and needles sensation.

From an early age I have been drawn to family pets and other animals, having a good connection with horses, pets, and now people. I continue to practice helping the horses, dogs, friends and family through absent healing, as well as using different types of crystal healing.

IN CONCLUSION

LOOKING BACK

Throughout my time in the racing community, there are a number of things I have been privileged to experience, have loved doing, and hope to continue, for example:

I cherish the opportunity I was given to learn to ride racehorses. Riding race horses allowed me live my dream of working in the equine industry and getting to know so many fine horses.

I learned to sense how to hold a strong horse on a gallop run, or to a steady canter. It's strange how this unexpectedly comes to you. One day you can't hold a horse, and the next day you acquire the right knack to hold them. Like when first learning to ride a bike, you try a few times before learning how to balance right, which then it becomes the natural thing to do.

I count it as a privilege to have lead up at races for three famous flat jockeys, and two 'champion' jump jockeys (champion jockey being the rider who has accumulated the most wins in one racing season). One of these had achieved champion jockey 3 times and another 11 times.

Had I not been in racing I would not have met a Manchester City player, who became a racehorse trainer. He kindly signed autographs for my Dad (a loyal football fan since his youth) and one for me too.

I have learnt many diverse things during my time in racing with one instance being Equine Healing, which led me to train as an Alternative Healer.

Despite all the challenges, I have never regretted making the decision to return to my passion. The many lovely opportunities and perks have far outweighed the small number of negatives. My love of working with horses hasn't diminished, rather it continues to grow. I get paid for doing something I really enjoy and that gift is priceless.

Chapter 15: Equine related terminology explained

(The following descriptions and explanations are based on my own equine experiences as well as from readily available free sources on the world wide web).

A
Astride: Riding with one leg on each side of the horse, other variations could be side saddle where the rider is seated with both legs to one side.

B
Barrel: Under belly of horse
Billet: A bar of metal that fits over the leather that goes round the bit that secures the reins to the bit
Bit: A type of horse tack used in equestrian activities, usually made of metal, or a synthetic material. It is placed in the mouth of a horse to assist a rider in communicating with the animal. It is held in place by means of a bridle and has reins attached for use by a rider.

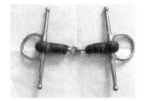

Blinkers/Visors:
Breaking In: The training of young horses …
Bridle: A piece of head equipment used to direct a horse. The 'bridle' includes both the headstall that holds a bit that goes in the mouth of a horse, and the reins that are attached to the bit.
Bridle headstall: Part of the rein that holds a bit that goes in the mouth of a horse.
Bucking: A movement performed by a horse or bull in which the animal lowers its head and raises its hindquarters into the air, usually while kicking out with the hind legs.

C
Canter: A measurement of speed of horse between a trot and a gallop. To canter is to ride a horse at a speed between a trot and a gallop, approx ? miles per hour.

Chamois: A type of soft, leather skin used for cleaning purposes buffing. Because it is not slip it is used to go under the saddle for the horses comfort.

Chifney Bit: An anti-rearing lead bit, gives the one leading it more control, as the mouthpiece, a thin metal circle, loops over the horses tongue. For example if a horse is nervous or very strong as it helps it to be led without incidents occurring. It can be severe so needs to be handled with care, if used at all.

Cinch (see Girth):

Colic: Abdominal pain caused by gastrointestinal conditions but not limited to. It can be caused by a change of diet, a lack of roughage or parasites. Mild cases generally respond well to pain relief and spasmolytic medications, such as Buscopan. Impaction colic: Is more serious as due to a blockage in the intestine. If left untreated and becomes severe, it can be fatal.

Colours: See Racing Colours

D

Dantian, dan t'ian, dan tien or tan t'ien: It is loosely translated as "elixir field", "sea of qi", or simply "energy centre". Dantian are the "qi focus flow centres", important focal points for meditative and exercise techniques such as qigong, martial arts such as t'ai chi ch'uan, and in traditional Chinese medicine..

Dressage: An equestrian sport defined by the International Equestrian Federation. Dressage is 'the highest expression of horse training' where horse and rider are expected to perform from memory a series of predetermined movements.

E

Endoscopy: (see also Gastroscopy) a clinical tool (brief decryption of this tool) is passed down into the stomach

Equestrian: Horse racing term for a person, horse, or vehicle for example used in a race or speed trial to set the pace. This doesn't sound right. I thought it meant horse-related??

Equine:

Equine Grooming: Daily horse grooming is an activity that enables the handler to check general health and well-being. Daily grooming improves the health and skin of the horses coat. As a minimum, grooming should be done before being worked, and after a workout.

F

False Start: Is when one horse (several) start before the signal is given. A horse for example might break through the starting gate before they open. There is usually no penalty, the horse is simply reloaded into the gate. In some events, however, a horse that breaks through the starting gate is disqualified. Similarly if a horse has broken through the starting gate and carries on round the track, and can't be returned to the stalls, it would be disqualified.

Flat: A contest, especially a race, where competitors are given an advantage or disadvantage of weight, distance, time, etc, in an attempt to equalise all entrants chances of winning.

Forelock/Foretop: Part of the horse's mane that grows from the animals poll (at the top of the horses head) and falls forward between the animal's ears and onto the forehead.

Furlong: A unit for measurement for distance. It is equal to 660 feet or 201.168 metres. There are 8 furlongs in a mile.

G

Gait: The pace of the horse. The so-called "natural" gaits, in increasing order of speed, are known as the walk, trot, canter, and gallop. In some animals the trot is replaced by the pace or an ambling gait. Horses who possess an ambling gait are usually also able to trot.

Gallop: The fastest speed at which a horse moves when all four feet are off the ground, or any fast pace. Speed approximately ?

Gastroscopy (Endoscopy): A method to diagnose gastric ulceration, a condition which can cause discomfort and poor per performance in horses.
Gastric ulceration can be caused by poor management when being exercised.

Gelding: Male horse that has been castrated.

Girth/Cinch: A piece of equipment used to keep the saddle in place on a horse or other animal. It passes under the barrel of the equine, usually attached to the saddle on both sides by two or three leather straps called billets.

H

Hack:(1) Verb: The act of riding a horse for light exercise, and (2) Noun: A type of horse used for riding out at ordinary speeds over roads and trails.

Head Collar and Rope:

Head lad/Yard Manager: The person in charge of managing the entire team of stable staff, and optimal yard working. Works closely with the Trainer daily to establish activities and allocate the over workload. These include breaking in young horses, monitoring the feeding regime, dealing with veterinary issues and carrying out medical treatments as directed by the vet).**Heat**: The temperature of the horses leg is higher than it would be normally after a workout or a race, or if the horse flinches when touched, it could be an indication of an underlying condition such as swelling or infection requiring an inspection by the vet.

Hoof pick: A hooked tool, usually of metal, used to clean out the hooves of a horse. A necessary task to remove foreign objects form the hooves.

Horse racing:
(1) Flat racing: Horses gallop directly between two points around a straight or oval track.
(2) Jump racing/Jumps racing: Also known as Steeplechasing/National Hunt racing: Horses race over obstacles.

Hunter: Term for a horse or pony with all the requisite traits for hunting.

Hunting: Searching out stags and foxes whilst on horseback, using hounds as trackers.

I

Impaction: the condition of being or process of becoming impacted, especially of faeces in the intestine.

J

Jockey: Horse race rider, primarily in a professional capacity. There are also amateur jockeys.

Jump horse: A competitive course over obstacles. Horses attempt a set course of obstacles one at a time, and are judged according to ability and speed to find the winner. Show jumping competition is an example

L

Laminitis: A disease affecting the feet and found mostly in horses and cattle. Early signs include foot tenderness progressing to inability to walk, increased digital pulses, and increased temperature in the hooves. A diet high in protein is often thought to contribute to conditions such as laminitis, colic, tying up and excitability.

Traumatic laminitis: is caused by repeated physical trauma to the feet during e.g. endurance riding, driving, or jumping on hard ground; it can also be caused by overenthusiastic hoof trimming. Severe lameness in one limb will cause a horse or pony to carry excessive weight on his other limbs, which may cause laminitis. Inflammatory Laminitis: A typical form of laminitis caused by inflammatory disease, is grain overload – For example if horses usually eat around 4 kg of straight starch-rich grain in *meal*, lowering this amount for horses not accustomed to eating a lot of grain, will reduce the risk.

Laminitis Prevention: Ensure the correct feed for each horse depending how much exercise it gets/energy it uses up. Getting horse nutrition correct is very important (see feed company's recommendations). Always turn horses out with at least one companion, and maintain a good exercise program to prevent obesity, To keep horses feet in best possible condition a farrier should check their feet regularly. Avoid hays that are known to have high levels of sugar, including ryegrass hay, oaten, wheaten or barley hay. Lucerne haylage or silage that has been produced specifically for horses is also a low sugar forage option.

Lead Rein (see Rein): Leather rein/strap to control and direct the horse's head let or right.

Length: A measurement of distance denoting the whole length of the horse (see also short head).

M

Mud fever (Dermatophilus congolensis and Staphylococcus spp): Also known as scratches or pastern dermatitis: A group of diseases horses can contract causing irritation and dermatitis in the lower limbs of horses. Often caused by a mixture of bacteria, but can also be caused by fungal organisms (dermatophytes). Horses should be kept in away from muddy conditions. In addition putting the horse on a walker will help to calm down the inflammation. The affected area should then be cleaned with a surgical scrub, antibacterial wash, rinsed off in warm water, and dried off, and finally hoof and heal cream applied.

N

Nose Bleed (epistaxis): Causes can range from wooden splinters caused whilst grazing or nuzzling. Other causes could be a knock to head or sinus infection. More serious causes could be due to exercised induced pulmonary haemorrhage which needs veterinary examination.

P

Paddock Sheet: A blanket put over a horse in the paddock

Plait: A hairstyle for the horses mane and may include a decorative yarn or braid interwoven with the horse hair, or other creative variations.

Point to Point: Is amateur steeple chase for horses used in hunting over a set cross-country course (a point to point meeting).

Pool money: The owner receives prize money for winning/placed runners. A percentage of the prize money is split between the trainer, the jockey, stable staff, and racing charities.

Pull mains: An action when combing out the horses main with the object of removing and thinning individual hair from the main, from the root, with the purpose of removing, shortening and thinning.

Q

Quarter Marks: Ornamentation on a horse seen in certain types of exhibition or competition In addition to highlighting the shine and health of the horse's coat, some designs are intended to help define the musculature of the horse or simply as an identifying or fun mark.

R

Racecourse Turf Surface:(1) Firm: Is a resilient racecourse turf surface.(2) Good: A racecourse turf surface slightly softer than firm.(3) Yielding: A racecourse. turf surface with a significant amount of 'give' to the ground caused by recent rain.(4) Soft: A racecourse turf surface with a large amount of moisture.

Racing Colours: Are the colours of the silk shirts worn by the jockeys when racing. The colours indicate the horses owner. The colours are looked after by the Jockey's valet until ready to wear them. They are part of the racing gear that is placed in the 'weight room'.

Rear Up: When a horse leans back on its hind legs and raise its front legs, assuming a threatening posture or avoiding something on the ground such as a snake. The rider is likely be suddenly thrown to the ground when this happens.

Rein: A pair of long straps (usually connected to the bit or the headpiece) used to control and direct the horse.

Reins: Items of horse tack, used to direct a horse or other animal used for riding. They are long straps that can be made of leather, nylon, metal, or other materials, and attach to a bridle via either its bit or its noseband.

Reins (Lead): Leather rein/strap to control and direct the horse's head left or right.

S

Saddle pad/blanket/numnah: A saddle cloth consisting of blankets, pads or fabrics inserted under a saddle. These are generally used to absorb sweat, cushion the saddle, and protect the horse's back

Sheet Pad see Paddock sheet:
Sheet Roller: Buckle and a strap that goes around the Paddock Sheet
Stirrup iron support consisting of metal loops into which rider's feet go. **stirrup**. saddle - a seat for the rider of a horse or camel.

Surcingle: A secondary girth
Sweat Sheet: A netted sheet that is placed over the horse during cooling down session after racing.

T
Tail Bandage: A bandage placed around the tail prior to racing to keep the horses tail clean
Travel Bandages: Bandages that go round the horses legs to protect them whilst travelling in the horse box
Travel Rug: A rug to keep the horse warm while travelling
Travel Rug Bag: A water-proof horse rug bag to keep the rugs clean and tidy
Trot: A two-beat diagonal gait of the horse where the diagonal pairs of legs move forward at the same time with a moment of suspension between each beat. A very slow trot is sometimes referred to as a jog

V
Visors see Blinkers:

W

Walker/Exerciser: A device to exercise horses or cool them down after training (hot walker).

Weight Cloth: A leather or material sack used to carry lead weights on a race horse as part of equalising a race.

Weight Room: Is where the jockey is weighed before and after each race.

Withers: The ridge between the shoulder blades of a horse. It is the standard place to measure the animal's height.

Work Rider: A term specific to racing, and used to describe anybody who can exercise ride a horse in training for a set piece of work. For example, a training session on the gallops, or schooling over fences at jump racing stables.

Y

Yard Manager/Head Lad: The person in charge of managing the entire team of stable staff, and optimal yard working. Works closely with the Trainer daily to establish activities and allocate the overall workload

Printed in Great Britain
by Amazon